50 Wholesome Breakfast Bowls for a Healthy Start

By: Kelly Johnson

Table of Contents

- Overnight Oats with Berries and Almonds
- Quinoa Breakfast Bowl with Banana and Maple Syrup
- Greek Yogurt Bowl with Honey and Walnuts
- Chia Seed Pudding with Coconut and Mango
- Savory Oatmeal Bowl with Spinach and Poached Egg
- Smoothie Bowl with Mixed Fruits and Granola
- Buckwheat Porridge with Apples and Cinnamon
- Avocado Toast Bowl with Cherry Tomatoes and Feta
- Peanut Butter Banana Overnight Oats
- Muesli Bowl with Yogurt and Fresh Fruit
- Cottage Cheese Bowl with Pineapple and Chia Seeds
- Sweet Potato Hash with Eggs and Avocado
- Acai Bowl with Granola and Coconut Flakes
- Raisin and Cinnamon Quinoa Bowl
- Egg and Veggie Breakfast Bowl with Salsa
- Breakfast Burrito Bowl with Black Beans and Avocado
- Berry and Nut Overnight Oats
- Granola Bowl with Almond Milk and Berries
- Savory Quinoa Bowl with Kale and Poached Egg
- Coconut Rice Pudding with Mango
- Maple Walnut Oatmeal Bowl
- Apple Cinnamon Chia Seed Pudding
- Egg and Sweet Potato Breakfast Bowl
- Berry Smoothie Bowl with Hemp Seeds
- Tofu Scramble Bowl with Spinach and Avocado
- Oatmeal Bowl with Peanut Butter and Sliced Banana
- Pineapple Coconut Quinoa Bowl
- Zucchini Noodle Bowl with Egg and Salsa
- Pumpkin Spice Oatmeal Bowl
- Peach Yogurt Bowl with Granola

- Mango and Coconut Chia Bowl
- Avocado and Egg Rice Bowl
- Almond Butter Banana Bowl with Oats
- Kefir Bowl with Mixed Berries and Flaxseed
- Nutty Quinoa Bowl with Apples and Almonds
- Spinach and Mushroom Breakfast Bowl
- Cacao Overnight Oats with Banana
- Savory Millet Bowl with Spinach and Egg
- Banana Berry Smoothie Bowl with Granola
- Cinnamon Roll Oatmeal Bowl
- Breakfast Couscous Bowl with Dried Fruit
- Egg and Avocado Toast Bowl
- Zesty Quinoa Bowl with Black Beans and Corn
- Oatmeal Bowl with Apples and Pecans
- Greek Yogurt Bowl with Fig and Pistachios
- Sweet Potato and Black Bean Breakfast Bowl
- Raspberry Almond Overnight Oats
- Spicy Tomato and Egg Breakfast Bowl
- Tropical Smoothie Bowl with Kiwi and Pineapple
- Savory Breakfast Bowl with Hummus and Veggies

Overnight Oats with Berries and Almonds

Ingredients:

- 1/2 cup rolled oats
- 1/2 cup almond milk (or your choice of milk)
- 1 tablespoon chia seeds
- 1/2 cup mixed berries
- 1 tablespoon sliced almonds
- 1 tablespoon honey or maple syrup (optional)

Instructions:

1. In a jar or bowl, combine oats, almond milk, chia seeds, and honey or maple syrup if using.
2. Stir well, cover, and refrigerate overnight.
3. In the morning, top with mixed berries and sliced almonds. Serve chilled.

Quinoa Breakfast Bowl with Banana and Maple Syrup

Ingredients:

- 1/2 cup cooked quinoa
- 1 banana, sliced
- 1 tablespoon maple syrup
- 1/4 cup almond milk (or your choice of milk)
- A sprinkle of cinnamon (optional)

Instructions:

1. Place cooked quinoa in a bowl and add almond milk.
2. Top with banana slices, drizzle with maple syrup, and sprinkle with cinnamon.
3. Serve warm or chilled.

Greek Yogurt Bowl with Honey and Walnuts

Ingredients:

- 1 cup Greek yogurt
- 1 tablespoon honey
- 2 tablespoons chopped walnuts
- 1/4 teaspoon ground cinnamon (optional)

Instructions:

1. In a bowl, add Greek yogurt.
2. Drizzle with honey, then top with chopped walnuts and a sprinkle of cinnamon if desired.
3. Serve immediately.

Chia Seed Pudding with Coconut and Mango

Ingredients:

- 1/4 cup chia seeds
- 1 cup coconut milk
- 1 tablespoon honey or maple syrup (optional)
- 1/2 cup fresh mango, diced

Instructions:

1. In a bowl, mix chia seeds, coconut milk, and honey or maple syrup if using.
2. Stir well, cover, and refrigerate for at least 4 hours or overnight.
3. Top with diced mango and serve chilled.

Savory Oatmeal Bowl with Spinach and Poached Egg

Ingredients:

- 1/2 cup rolled oats
- 1 cup vegetable broth (or water)
- 1/2 cup fresh spinach
- 1 poached egg
- Salt and pepper to taste

Instructions:

1. Cook oats in vegetable broth according to package instructions.
2. In the last minute of cooking, stir in spinach until wilted.
3. Top the oatmeal with a poached egg and season with salt and pepper.
4. Serve warm.

Smoothie Bowl with Mixed Fruits and Granola

Ingredients:

- 1 banana
- 1/2 cup mixed berries (fresh or frozen)
- 1/2 cup almond milk (or your choice of milk)
- 1/4 cup granola
- 1/4 cup sliced fresh fruits (like kiwi, strawberries, or mango)

Instructions:

1. In a blender, combine banana, mixed berries, and almond milk. Blend until smooth.
2. Pour into a bowl and top with granola and sliced fresh fruits.
3. Serve immediately.

Buckwheat Porridge with Apples and Cinnamon

Ingredients:

- 1/2 cup buckwheat groats
- 1 cup almond milk (or your choice of milk)
- 1/2 apple, diced
- 1/2 teaspoon ground cinnamon
- 1 tablespoon maple syrup (optional)

Instructions:

1. Cook buckwheat groats in almond milk according to package instructions.
2. Once cooked, stir in diced apples, cinnamon, and maple syrup if using.
3. Serve warm, garnished with a sprinkle of cinnamon and extra apple slices.

Enjoy these wholesome and nourishing breakfast bowls!

Avocado Toast Bowl with Cherry Tomatoes and Feta

Ingredients:

- 1 avocado, mashed
- 1/2 cup cherry tomatoes, halved
- 2 tablespoons crumbled feta cheese
- 1 slice whole-grain bread, toasted and cut into bite-sized pieces
- 1 tablespoon olive oil
- Salt and pepper to taste

Instructions:

1. In a bowl, mix mashed avocado, cherry tomatoes, and feta.
2. Drizzle with olive oil, season with salt and pepper, and add the toasted bread pieces.
3. Toss gently and serve immediately.

Peanut Butter Banana Overnight Oats

Ingredients:

- 1/2 cup rolled oats
- 1/2 cup almond milk (or your choice of milk)
- 1 tablespoon peanut butter
- 1 banana, sliced
- 1 teaspoon honey (optional)

Instructions:

1. In a jar or bowl, combine oats, almond milk, peanut butter, and honey if using.
2. Stir well, cover, and refrigerate overnight.
3. In the morning, top with banana slices and serve chilled.

Muesli Bowl with Yogurt and Fresh Fruit

Ingredients:

- 1/2 cup muesli
- 1 cup Greek yogurt
- 1/4 cup mixed fresh fruit (like berries, kiwi, or mango)
- 1 tablespoon honey or maple syrup (optional)

Instructions:

1. In a bowl, combine muesli and Greek yogurt.
2. Top with fresh fruit and drizzle with honey or maple syrup if desired.
3. Serve immediately.

Cottage Cheese Bowl with Pineapple and Chia Seeds

Ingredients:

- 1 cup cottage cheese
- 1/2 cup fresh pineapple, diced
- 1 tablespoon chia seeds
- 1 teaspoon honey (optional)

Instructions:

1. In a bowl, add cottage cheese and top with pineapple and chia seeds.
2. Drizzle with honey if desired.
3. Serve immediately.

Sweet Potato Hash with Eggs and Avocado

Ingredients:

- 1 medium sweet potato, peeled and diced
- 2 eggs
- 1/2 avocado, sliced
- 1 tablespoon olive oil
- Salt and pepper to taste

Instructions:

1. Heat olive oil in a skillet over medium heat. Add diced sweet potatoes and cook until tender and slightly crispy, about 10-12 minutes.
2. In a separate pan, cook eggs to your liking (fried or scrambled).
3. Serve the sweet potato hash topped with eggs and sliced avocado. Season with salt and pepper.

Acai Bowl with Granola and Coconut Flakes

Ingredients:

- 1 acai puree packet (frozen)
- 1 banana
- 1/2 cup mixed berries
- 1/2 cup almond milk (or your choice of milk)
- 1/4 cup granola
- 1 tablespoon coconut flakes

Instructions:

1. In a blender, combine acai puree, banana, mixed berries, and almond milk. Blend until smooth.
2. Pour into a bowl and top with granola and coconut flakes.
3. Serve immediately.

Raisin and Cinnamon Quinoa Bowl

Ingredients:

- 1/2 cup cooked quinoa
- 1 tablespoon raisins
- 1/2 teaspoon ground cinnamon
- 1 tablespoon maple syrup (optional)
- 1/4 cup almond milk (or your choice of milk)

Instructions:

1. In a bowl, combine cooked quinoa, raisins, cinnamon, and maple syrup if using.
2. Pour in almond milk and stir to combine.
3. Serve warm or chilled, garnished with a sprinkle of cinnamon.

Enjoy these nutritious and flavorful breakfast bowls!

Egg and Veggie Breakfast Bowl with Salsa

Ingredients:

- 2 eggs, scrambled
- 1/2 cup cooked spinach
- 1/4 cup sautéed bell peppers
- 1/4 avocado, sliced
- 2 tablespoons salsa
- Salt and pepper to taste

Instructions:

1. In a bowl, add scrambled eggs, cooked spinach, sautéed bell peppers, and avocado slices.
2. Top with salsa and season with salt and pepper.
3. Serve immediately.

Breakfast Burrito Bowl with Black Beans and Avocado

Ingredients:

- 1/2 cup cooked black beans
- 1/2 avocado, diced
- 1/4 cup salsa
- 2 scrambled eggs
- 1/4 cup shredded cheddar cheese
- 1/4 cup cooked brown rice (optional)

Instructions:

1. In a bowl, layer scrambled eggs, black beans, avocado, and brown rice (if using).
2. Top with salsa and shredded cheese.
3. Serve warm.

Berry and Nut Overnight Oats

Ingredients:

- 1/2 cup rolled oats
- 1/2 cup almond milk (or your choice of milk)
- 1/4 cup mixed berries
- 1 tablespoon chopped nuts (like almonds or walnuts)
- 1 tablespoon honey (optional)

Instructions:

1. In a jar or bowl, combine oats, almond milk, and honey if using.
2. Stir well, cover, and refrigerate overnight.
3. In the morning, top with mixed berries and chopped nuts. Serve chilled.

Granola Bowl with Almond Milk and Berries

Ingredients:

- 1/2 cup granola
- 1/2 cup almond milk (or your choice of milk)
- 1/4 cup mixed berries

Instructions:

1. In a bowl, add granola and pour almond milk over it.
2. Top with mixed berries.
3. Serve immediately.

Savory Quinoa Bowl with Kale and Poached Egg

Ingredients:

- 1/2 cup cooked quinoa
- 1/2 cup sautéed kale
- 1 poached egg
- 1 tablespoon olive oil
- Salt and pepper to taste

Instructions:

1. In a bowl, place cooked quinoa and top with sautéed kale.
2. Add the poached egg on top, drizzle with olive oil, and season with salt and pepper.
3. Serve warm.

Coconut Rice Pudding with Mango

Ingredients:

- 1/2 cup cooked jasmine rice
- 1/2 cup coconut milk
- 1 tablespoon honey or maple syrup
- 1/4 cup fresh mango, diced

Instructions:

1. In a saucepan, combine cooked jasmine rice, coconut milk, and honey or maple syrup. Simmer for 5-7 minutes until thickened.
2. Serve topped with fresh mango.

Maple Walnut Oatmeal Bowl

Ingredients:

- 1/2 cup rolled oats
- 1 cup almond milk (or your choice of milk)
- 1 tablespoon maple syrup
- 2 tablespoons chopped walnuts
- A pinch of ground cinnamon

Instructions:

1. Cook oats in almond milk according to package instructions.
2. Stir in maple syrup and top with chopped walnuts and cinnamon.
3. Serve warm.

Apple Cinnamon Chia Seed Pudding

Ingredients:

- 1/4 cup chia seeds
- 1 cup almond milk (or your choice of milk)
- 1/4 teaspoon ground cinnamon
- 1/2 apple, diced
- 1 tablespoon honey or maple syrup (optional)

Instructions:

1. In a bowl, mix chia seeds, almond milk, cinnamon, and honey or maple syrup if using.
2. Stir well, cover, and refrigerate for at least 4 hours or overnight.
3. Top with diced apple before serving.

Enjoy these delicious and balanced breakfast bowls!

Egg and Sweet Potato Breakfast Bowl

Ingredients:

- 1 medium sweet potato, peeled and diced
- 2 eggs, scrambled or fried
- 1/4 avocado, sliced
- 1 tablespoon olive oil
- Salt and pepper to taste

Instructions:

1. Heat olive oil in a skillet over medium heat. Cook diced sweet potatoes until tender and golden, about 10-12 minutes.
2. In a separate pan, cook eggs to your liking.
3. In a bowl, combine sweet potatoes, eggs, and avocado slices. Season with salt and pepper. Serve warm.

Berry Smoothie Bowl with Hemp Seeds

Ingredients:

- 1/2 cup mixed frozen berries
- 1/2 banana
- 1/2 cup almond milk (or your choice of milk)
- 1 tablespoon hemp seeds
- 1/4 cup granola

Instructions:

1. Blend mixed berries, banana, and almond milk until smooth.
2. Pour into a bowl and top with hemp seeds and granola.
3. Serve immediately.

Tofu Scramble Bowl with Spinach and Avocado

Ingredients:

- 1/2 block firm tofu, crumbled
- 1/2 cup spinach, sautéed
- 1/4 avocado, sliced
- 1 tablespoon olive oil
- 1/4 teaspoon turmeric
- Salt and pepper to taste

Instructions:

1. Heat olive oil in a pan and add crumbled tofu. Season with turmeric, salt, and pepper. Cook for 5-7 minutes.
2. In a bowl, combine tofu scramble, sautéed spinach, and avocado slices.
3. Serve warm.

Oatmeal Bowl with Peanut Butter and Sliced Banana

Ingredients:

- 1/2 cup rolled oats
- 1 cup almond milk (or your choice of milk)
- 1 tablespoon peanut butter
- 1 banana, sliced
- 1 tablespoon honey (optional)

Instructions:

1. Cook oats in almond milk according to package instructions.
2. Top with peanut butter, banana slices, and honey if desired.
3. Serve warm.

Pineapple Coconut Quinoa Bowl

Ingredients:

- 1/2 cup cooked quinoa
- 1/4 cup fresh pineapple, diced
- 1/4 cup coconut milk
- 1 tablespoon shredded coconut

Instructions:

1. In a bowl, combine cooked quinoa and diced pineapple.
2. Drizzle with coconut milk and sprinkle with shredded coconut.
3. Serve chilled or at room temperature.

Zucchini Noodle Bowl with Egg and Salsa

Ingredients:

- 1 medium zucchini, spiralized
- 1 egg, poached or fried
- 2 tablespoons salsa
- 1 tablespoon olive oil
- Salt and pepper to taste

Instructions:

1. Heat olive oil in a pan and sauté zucchini noodles for 2-3 minutes until tender.
2. In a bowl, add zucchini noodles and top with the egg and salsa.
3. Season with salt and pepper and serve immediately.

Pumpkin Spice Oatmeal Bowl

Ingredients:

- 1/2 cup rolled oats
- 1 cup almond milk (or your choice of milk)
- 1/4 cup pumpkin puree
- 1/2 teaspoon pumpkin spice
- 1 tablespoon maple syrup

Instructions:

1. Cook oats in almond milk according to package instructions. Stir in pumpkin puree and pumpkin spice.
2. Drizzle with maple syrup and serve warm.

Enjoy these delicious and nutritious breakfast bowls!

Peach Yogurt Bowl with Granola

Ingredients:

- 1/2 cup Greek yogurt
- 1 ripe peach, sliced
- 1/4 cup granola
- 1 tablespoon honey (optional)

Instructions:

1. In a bowl, add Greek yogurt and top with sliced peaches and granola.
2. Drizzle with honey if desired and serve immediately.

Mango and Coconut Chia Bowl

Ingredients:

- 1/4 cup chia seeds
- 1 cup coconut milk
- 1/2 ripe mango, diced
- 1 tablespoon shredded coconut

Instructions:

1. In a bowl, mix chia seeds and coconut milk. Refrigerate for 4 hours or overnight.
2. Top with diced mango and shredded coconut before serving.

Avocado and Egg Rice Bowl

Ingredients:

- 1/2 cup cooked brown rice
- 1/2 avocado, sliced
- 1 poached or fried egg
- 1 tablespoon soy sauce or tamari
- Salt and pepper to taste

Instructions:

1. In a bowl, add cooked rice, avocado slices, and the egg.
2. Drizzle with soy sauce or tamari and season with salt and pepper.
3. Serve warm.

Almond Butter Banana Bowl with Oats

Ingredients:

- 1/2 cup rolled oats
- 1 cup almond milk (or your choice of milk)
- 1 banana, sliced
- 1 tablespoon almond butter

Instructions:

1. Cook oats in almond milk according to package instructions.
2. Top with sliced banana and drizzle almond butter on top. Serve warm.

Kefir Bowl with Mixed Berries and Flaxseed

Ingredients:

- 1/2 cup kefir
- 1/4 cup mixed berries (blueberries, raspberries, etc.)
- 1 tablespoon ground flaxseed
- 1 tablespoon honey (optional)

Instructions:

1. In a bowl, pour kefir and top with mixed berries and ground flaxseed.
2. Drizzle with honey if desired and serve immediately.

Nutty Quinoa Bowl with Apples and Almonds

Ingredients:

- 1/2 cup cooked quinoa
- 1/2 apple, diced
- 2 tablespoons almonds, chopped
- 1 tablespoon honey or maple syrup

Instructions:

1. In a bowl, combine cooked quinoa, diced apple, and chopped almonds.
2. Drizzle with honey or maple syrup and serve warm or chilled.

Nutty Quinoa Bowl with Apples and Almonds

Spinach and Mushroom Breakfast Bowl

Ingredients:

- 1/2 cup sautéed spinach
- 1/2 cup sautéed mushrooms
- 2 scrambled eggs
- 1 tablespoon olive oil
- Salt and pepper to taste

Instructions:

1. In a skillet, sauté spinach and mushrooms in olive oil until tender.
2. In a bowl, add scrambled eggs and top with sautéed spinach and mushrooms.
3. Season with salt and pepper and serve warm.

Enjoy these flavorful and healthy breakfast bowls!

Cacao Overnight Oats with Banana

Ingredients:

- 1/2 cup rolled oats
- 1 tablespoon cacao powder
- 1 cup almond milk (or your choice of milk)
- 1 banana, sliced
- 1 tablespoon chia seeds (optional)

Instructions:

1. In a jar, mix oats, cacao powder, almond milk, and chia seeds. Refrigerate overnight.
2. In the morning, top with banana slices and serve chilled.

Savory Millet Bowl with Spinach and Egg

Ingredients:

- 1/2 cup cooked millet
- 1/2 cup sautéed spinach
- 1 fried or poached egg
- 1 tablespoon olive oil
- Salt and pepper to taste

Instructions:

1. In a bowl, add cooked millet and sautéed spinach.
2. Top with the fried egg, drizzle with olive oil, and season with salt and pepper. Serve warm.

Banana Berry Smoothie Bowl with Granola

Ingredients:

- 1/2 banana
- 1/2 cup mixed berries
- 1/2 cup almond milk (or your choice of milk)
- 1/4 cup granola

Instructions:

1. Blend banana, mixed berries, and almond milk until smooth.
2. Pour into a bowl and top with granola. Serve immediately.

Cinnamon Roll Oatmeal Bowl

Ingredients:

- 1/2 cup rolled oats
- 1 cup almond milk (or your choice of milk)
- 1/2 teaspoon cinnamon
- 1 tablespoon maple syrup

Instructions:

1. Cook oats in almond milk according to package instructions. Stir in cinnamon and maple syrup.
2. Serve warm, adding extra cinnamon or syrup if desired.

Breakfast Couscous Bowl with Dried Fruit

Ingredients:

- 1/2 cup couscous
- 1/4 cup mixed dried fruit (raisins, apricots, etc.)
- 1 tablespoon honey
- 1/2 cup almond milk (or your choice of milk)

Instructions:

1. Cook couscous according to package instructions, using almond milk instead of water.
2. Stir in dried fruit and honey. Serve warm or chilled.

Egg and Avocado Toast Bowl

Ingredients:

- 1 slice whole-grain bread, toasted and cut into pieces
- 1/2 avocado, mashed
- 1 fried or poached egg
- Salt and pepper to taste

Instructions:

1. In a bowl, add the toasted bread pieces and top with mashed avocado and the fried egg.
2. Season with salt and pepper. Serve immediately.

Zesty Quinoa Bowl with Black Beans and Corn

Ingredients:

- 1/2 cup cooked quinoa
- 1/4 cup black beans
- 1/4 cup corn kernels
- 1 tablespoon lime juice
- 1 tablespoon chopped cilantro
- Salt and pepper to taste

Instructions:

1. In a bowl, combine cooked quinoa, black beans, and corn.
2. Drizzle with lime juice, sprinkle cilantro, and season with salt and pepper. Serve warm or chilled.

These bowls are perfect for a healthy and filling start to your day!

Oatmeal Bowl with Apples and Pecans

Ingredients:

- 1/2 cup rolled oats
- 1 cup almond milk (or your choice of milk)
- 1/2 apple, diced
- 2 tablespoons chopped pecans
- 1 tablespoon maple syrup

Instructions:

1. Cook oats in almond milk according to package instructions.
2. Top with diced apple, chopped pecans, and drizzle with maple syrup. Serve warm.

Greek Yogurt Bowl with Fig and Pistachios

Ingredients:

- 1/2 cup Greek yogurt
- 2 fresh figs, sliced
- 2 tablespoons pistachios, chopped
- 1 tablespoon honey (optional)

Instructions:

1. In a bowl, add Greek yogurt and top with sliced figs and chopped pistachios.
2. Drizzle with honey if desired and serve immediately.

Sweet Potato and Black Bean Breakfast Bowl

Ingredients:

- 1/2 cup roasted sweet potatoes
- 1/4 cup black beans
- 1 poached egg
- 1 tablespoon salsa
- Salt and pepper to taste

Instructions:

1. In a bowl, combine roasted sweet potatoes and black beans.
2. Top with a poached egg and a spoonful of salsa. Season with salt and pepper and serve warm.

Raspberry Almond Overnight Oats

Ingredients:

- 1/2 cup rolled oats
- 1/2 cup almond milk (or your choice of milk)
- 1/4 cup raspberries
- 1 tablespoon almond butter

Instructions:

1. In a jar, mix oats and almond milk. Refrigerate overnight.
2. In the morning, top with raspberries and drizzle with almond butter. Serve chilled.

Spicy Tomato and Egg Breakfast Bowl

Ingredients:

- 1/2 cup cooked quinoa
- 1 poached egg
- 1/4 cup spicy tomato sauce
- 1 tablespoon chopped cilantro
- Salt and pepper to taste

Instructions:

1. In a bowl, add cooked quinoa and top with a poached egg.
2. Pour spicy tomato sauce over the egg and sprinkle with cilantro. Season with salt and pepper and serve warm.

Tropical Smoothie Bowl with Kiwi and Pineapple

Ingredients:

- 1/2 cup frozen pineapple chunks
- 1/2 kiwi, sliced
- 1/2 banana
- 1/2 cup coconut water
- 1/4 cup granola

Instructions:

1. Blend frozen pineapple, banana, and coconut water until smooth.
2. Pour into a bowl and top with kiwi slices and granola. Serve immediately.

Savory Breakfast Bowl with Hummus and Veggies

Ingredients:

- 1/2 cup cooked quinoa
- 2 tablespoons hummus
- 1/4 cup cherry tomatoes, halved
- 1/4 cup cucumber, diced
- 1 poached egg
- Salt and pepper to taste

Instructions:

1. In a bowl, add cooked quinoa and top with hummus, cherry tomatoes, cucumber, and poached egg.
2. Season with salt and pepper and serve warm.

These bowls offer a variety of flavors and textures, perfect for breakfast!